CODE BREAKERS AND SPIES

Code Breakers and Spies of World War II

CATHLEEN SMALL

Cavendish Square
New York

Published in 2019 by Cavendish Square Publishing, LLC
243 5th Avenue, Suite 136, New York, NY 10016

First Edition

Library of Congress Cataloging-in-Publication Data

Names: Small, Cathleen, author.
Title: Code breakers and spies of World War II / Cathleen Small.
Description: First edition. | New York : Cavendish Square, 2018. | Series: Code breakers and spies | Includes bibliographical references and index. | Audience: Grade 7 to 12.
Identifiers: LCCN 2017058831 (print) | LCCN 2017059320 (ebook) | ISBN 9781502638557 (eBook) | ISBN 9781502638533 (library bound : alk. paper) | ISBN 9781502638540 (pbk. : alk. paper)
Subjects: LCSH: World War, 1939-1945--Secret service--Juvenile literature. | Espionage--History--20th century--Juvenile literature. | Spies--History--20th century--Juvenile literature.
Classification: LCC D810.S7 (ebook) | LCC D810. S7 S5534 2018 (print) | DDC 940.54/85--dc23
LC record available at https://lccn.loc.gov/2017058831

Editorial Director: David McNamara
Editor: Stacy Orlando
Copy Editor: Alex Tessman
Associate Art Director: Amy Greenan
Designer: Joe Parenteau
Production Coordinator: Karol Szymczuk
Photo Research: J8 Media

The photographs in this book are used by permission and through the courtesy of: Cover Brian Harris/Alamy Stock Photo; p. 4, 32, 48 Corbis/Getty Images; p. 7 Stock Montage/Getty Images; p. 11 Timothy H. O'Sullivan/Buyenlarge/Getty Images; p. 15 Apic/Getty Images; p. 20 Steve Simmons/Alamy Stock Photo; p. 24 Rex Features/AP Images; p. 30, 42, 47 SSPL/Getty Images; p. 34 Library of Congress; p. 38 Culture Club/Getty Images; p. 44 Evening Standard/Getty Images; p. 54 Bettmann/Getty Images; p. 57 DPA Picture Alliance/Alamy Stock Photo; p. 60 Sovfoto/UIG/Getty Images; p. 62 Ian Dagnall Computing/Alamy Stock Photo; p. 64 G.B. Kress/Bettmann/Getty Images; p. 66 Philippe Turpin/Photononstop/Getty Images.

Printed in the United States of America

Contents

CHAPTER 1

THE EVOLUTION OF ESPIONAGE

Today, espionage brings to mind popular news stories over the past few years; for instance, the 2017 accusations of Americans colluding with Russians, Russians interfering with the 2016 presidential election, multiple instances of leaked or deleted emails, and classified documents released through sites like WikiLeaks. Yet espionage is nothing new. In fact, spying has been around for centuries.

Early efforts of spies and code breakers may have involved simple methods of espionage, but they impacted many events over the course of history.

OPPOSITE: During the Civil War, hot-air balloons were one form of surveillance technology used on the battlefield.

Queen Elizabeth I of England, for example, had a spymaster named Francis Walsingham in the sixteenth century. Walsingham uncovered a plot by Mary, Queen of Scots, for a Catholic rebellion that would lead to Queen Elizabeth's assassination and Mary's ascension to the throne. During the American Revolution, Lydia Darragh overheard British officers planning to attack American soldiers a few days later, and she sent word to American forces. The information helped prevent the attack from taking place. Ciphers created by Charles Wheatstone of England in the 1800s were utilized by many militaries for years, including in World War I and World War II. By the time of the American Civil War, both technique and technology became more advanced.

Spying during the Civil War

At the outbreak of the Civil War, neither side had centralized intelligence agencies, but gathering information would provide necessary tactical advantages. Espionage techniques during the conflict employed a wide range of methods, from simple strategies such as using women as spies, to more technological advancements such as telegraphs and hot-air balloons.

Women Undercover

Women proved to be effective spies during the Civil War. At the time, women were generally seen simply as wives and mothers, who stayed home and cooked. People didn't expect females to be spies. Often the presence of women was ignored, allowing them to eavesdrop on otherwise confidential conversations. Women could also pretend to be unmarried women

Major Pauline Cushman was a spy for the Union army during the Civil War.

or grieving widows, and flirt with military officials to gain access to secret information. Some would even go undercover and dress as men both to serve on the battlefields and to gain information.

Ciphers

Civil War spies also used ciphers to translate coded messages. A cipher is another name for a code. Often ciphers involve substituting symbols for letters of the alphabet. The simplest cipher involves assigning a number to each letter of the alphabet: 1 for A, 2 for B, 3 for C, and so on. An official might receive a message that looked like this:

2 18 9 20 9 19 8   1 20 20 1 3 11

Knowing that the simple letter-for-number cipher was used, they could translate that to read:

British   attack

This would be considered an incredibly straightforward cipher that anyone could quickly decode. In fact, ciphers like these are referred to as simple substitution, because of the basic one-to-one correspondence of letters to symbols. Sometimes, the symbols are simply other letters, such as M substituted for A; N substituted for B; and so on. While simple substitutions were used in some Civil War ciphers, most ciphers were much tougher to crack. The idea is the same: symbols stand for letters or words, and the coded message can be decoded as long as the recipient knows the key.

Confederate President Jefferson Davis created a dictionary code to be used during the Civil War. To designate a word, the person writing the code would write the page number; either L, M, or R to designate the left, middle, or right column on the page; and the number of the word counting from the top of the page. So, for example, the code for a particular word might look like: 153,M,17. The Navy used a similar dictionary code, though it did not designate columns and instead included the page number and the number of the word on the page, looking something like (473)24 for each word.

Route transposition was also utilized, where the words in the cipher were written in a matrix, line by line, and in order to crack the code the words need to be read in columns, following a certain route. In most modern languages, text is read horizontally left to right, and sometimes right to left, but very rarely in vertical columns – certainly not skipping around the page. Ciphers like these are much harder to crack.

The First Industrial War

Cryptography and ciphers helped keep information secret in the event a message was intercepted, which could happen quite often with the old ways of delivering written correspondence. Messengers would use common goods with false bottoms and hidden compartments, and women could even smuggle notes in their skirts, but people traveling on foot or horseback could be captured by the enemy. Advancements and inventions during the nineteenth century brought about a vast number of improvements in many industries. These technological advancements lead to better and faster ways to communicate and travel during the Civil War.

The Telegraph

President Abraham Lincoln used the electric telegraph to communicate with troops and receive updates. This enabled soldiers in the North to be far more prepared than Confederate soldiers, who did not have large-scale operations like the Union Army's US Military Telegraph Corps. Established in 1861 and led by Andrew Carnegie, the corps strung 4,000 miles of telegraph wire, trained more than twelve hundred operators, and sent more than

The US Military Telegraph Corps handled more than a million telegraph messages during the Civil War.

a million messages to and from the battlefields in the first year alone.

The telegraph is essentially a code transmission device. Messages sent by telegraph are in Morse code, a series of dots and dashes developed by Samuel Morse in the 1830s and 1840s. This code is tapped in via an operator key that is pressed down to transmit an electrical pulse that is then sent over wires. Telegraph operators on the receiving end would receive the series of dots and dashes and translate them into letters and words. For example, one popular Morse code transmission is the distress call SOS, for Save Our

Ship. S is designated by three dots, or short electrical pulses. O is designated by three long dashes, or long electrical pulses. So the Morse code tapped into the telegraph for SOS was *dot dot dot dash dash dash dot dot dot*.

Hot-Air Balloons

Airplanes had not yet been invented during the Civil War, but short-distance air travel was possible in hot-air balloons. The military realized that hot-air balloons could also be used for surveillance. In 1861, the Union army sent Thaddeus Lowe up in a hot-air balloon to spy on Confederate troops stationed in Falls Church, Virginia, just a couple of miles away. Lowe sent intelligence about the Confederate soldiers via telegraph, which the Union army used to attack Confederate targets. It took almost another year before the Confederate army caught up to the Union army in using hot-air balloon technology for espionage.

Spy Craft of World War I

Technology continued to develop after the Civil War, and by the time World War I came around in the early twentieth century, new inventions and scientific advancements were in place and industry provided additional avenues for agents. Old methods employed by spies were still used, just in new and creative ways.

Morse Code Devices

During World War I, Morse code was used to transmit messages with other devices besides the telegraph. For example, steam locomotive engineers in Belgium realized if they opened and closed the fireboxes in locomotives in the pattern of dots and dashes, the steam emitted from the locomotive would appear in a series of short puffs (dots) and long puffs (dashes). They used this system to transmit messages to British troops in Holland. Similarly, German agents used the "sails" of Dutch windmills to transmit messages via Morse code. They would use a series of starts and stops to the windmill's motion to transmit their code.

Consumer Communications

Spies in World War I also realized consumer goods could provide new avenues for hiding information in plain sight. One German agent pretended to be a merchant shipping sardines to Peru, and he concealed messages about British shipping movements in between sardine invoices. It took a while before British agents thought to look through a

Mata Hari: The Seductress Spy

Margaretha Geertruida "Margreet" MacLeod was a Dutch exotic dancer who went by the stage name Mata Hari. Being a dancer from the Netherlands, a neutral country during World War I, Mata Hari was allowed to travel where others would not otherwise be able. It was the perfect cover. She was quite famous, and naturally would need to travel to other countries in order to perform for her very influential and powerful fans. One such admirer was Crown Prince Wilhelm, for whom Mata Hari had performed a few times before the war.

The prince also happened to be the eldest son of Kaiser Wilhelm II, a senior German general. Mata Hari was quite attractive, and openly displayed her body in her performances. She also had a reputation for being flirtatious and promiscuous, a fact recognized by the Deuxième Bureau, a French military intelligence agency. The Bureau met Mata Hari as she attempted to visit her wounded lover, and insisted that she could only see him if she agreed to spy on Germany. The plan was for her to seduce Crown Prince Wilhelm and gain intelligence about German plans. Mata Hari agreed to do it, but she reportedly later turned on the Bureau and became a double agent, agreeing to sell French secrets to Germany.

Intercepted radio transmissions eventually led to her downfall, and she was charged with being a German spy. Mata Hari was convicted of espionage and executed in 1917, with many insisting she had used her powers of seduction to manipulate men and gain intelligence. During interrogations she maintained that though she took money from the Germans, she was always loyal to France. Some think she was a pawn of both countries, who took advantage of her financial situation and position. The truth, of course, died with Mata Hari and the people who commissioned her.

The beautiful Mata Hari was a Dutch dancer who doubled as a German spy during World War I.

bunch of sardine invoices for any sort of intelligence being transmitted.

German agents posed as cigar merchants and placed large orders for cigars. In reality, the brands and sizes of cigars ordered were coded messages about the ships in the harbor. The plan fell apart when the British realized the cigar orders were unrealistically large, given that most British soldiers smoked pipes and cigarettes, not cigars. Other German agents in Moscow used bread displays in a bakery window to transmit messages to spies, and used certain patterns and combinations of the bread and dates in the display to communicate.

Listening Technology

Espionage wasn't all reboots of old techniques, though. New technologies were put to use in the military as well. For example, the Germans developed the Moritz, a device that let them intercept messages from British field telephones. German soldiers buried copper plates in the ground near the phone lines used for British field telephones. When connected to the Moritz, the plates amplified the current coming through the phone lines and allowed German spies to wear headphones that let them listen to Allied communications.

It was clever technology, but it only worked as long as the Allied soldiers didn't realize it existed. Once the Allies learned about the Moritz, they began speaking in code. German spies using the Moritz could still hear them, but they now had to break the code too.

New Codes

Ciphers had been around for a while by World War I, and some of the ciphers from earlier days had been cracked. The military needed new and tougher codes to use. One effective method was code talking done by Native Americans. Soldiers from the Choctaw, Cherokee, Cheyenne, and Comanche tribes would transmit messages in code based on their native tongue, and since very few people outside the tribes knew the language, spies listening in could not translate the information. Native Americans would also prove to be instrumental in World War II.

Spy Aircraft

Airplane flight was in its infancy at the dawn of the twentieth century. The Wright Brothers had only pioneered the first sustained and controlled heavier-than-air powered flight in 1903. Hot-air balloons were still in use for surveillance, and so were dirigibles, like the German zeppelins. However, during

World War I there were planes in the air, and the military put the technology to use both for bombing and reconnaissance.

Sometimes pilots would use handheld cameras to take surveillance photos, but not in general practice at first, as they were rather heavy, unwieldy, and difficult to operate in the air. Often the pilots simply looked over the area and then wrote down their observations after they landed.

If a message needed to be transmitted more quickly, pilots would perform aerial maneuvers to get information to those on the ground. Sometimes aviators would drop colored flares to send a message. The French and British ultimately developed radio transmitters that made communication much easier.

DID YOU KNOW?

Dirigibles, which can provide 360-degree radar coverage twenty-four hours a day for up to thirty days at a time, are still used today for surveillance because the cost is significantly lower than using modern aircraft.

Later, camera technology improved and resulted in lighter, more accurate cameras that could be used in aircraft surveillance; such technologies were pioneered by the German, Austrian, and French militaries. The United States was not far behind in technology, though, and the US Army Corps of Engineers soon developed aerial cameras as well. When the United States entered World War I in 1917, US Air Force photographers learned from the British, and US School of Aerial Photography was established in 1918.

Dirigibles and balloons were both lighter-than-air aircraft, which meant they couldn't hold much weight, such as excess cameras. When fixed-wing aircraft were developed, it meant more flexibility in the equipment that could be mounted in an aircraft, such as more advanced cameras and radios.

The time up to World War II certainly provided many developments in spy technology and techniques, and advancements continued in the 1930s and 1940s as war broke out and battles waged between the Axis and the Allies.

CHAPTER 2

SPYING AND TECHNOLOGY IN WORLD WAR II

World War II was a long and bloody war, with mass casualties on both sides. The deadliest period in human history was also a fascinating time in the development of cryptography and spy technology. While spy movies like the James Bond series might seem a little farfetched, in reality some of the technologies developed from 1939 to 1945 were just like something out of a movie.

OPPOSITE:
During World War II, Bletchley Park was home to massive computer systems like this.

Spy Weaponry

Undercover operatives could not carry obvious weapons without the risk of being detected, so agencies dedicated resources to the development of specialized arms. Pipe pistols, rodent bombs, poison tablets and cigarettes, and grenades disguised as lumps of coal all were among the inventions during the war. While not all efforts worked, a few were successful staples for spies.

Silencers

Gun silencers, or suppressors, were invented in the early twentieth century but were not used extensively until World War II. Initially designed mainly to help protect against the loud reports of gunshots, which could damage hearing, silencers also proved useful if a person needed to discreetly shoot another person. The United States Office of Strategic Services (OSS), an intelligence agency formed in 1942, researched and produced its own line of spy tools including a silencer reportedly used with High Standard HDM .22 Long Rifle pistols.

Of course, not all agents needed silencers since spying was focused on transmitting sensitive information rather than killing. But if an agent needed to take a shot, silencers were helpful to remain unnoticed.

Hidden Daggers

Another silent weapon of protection among spies were assassination daggers disguised as fountain pens, lapel pins, and similar insignificant objects. The daggers had to be small and sharp in order to be concealed; however, they proved to be deadly little weapons. Agents could use the instruments to take down Nazi guards and others who posed a threat to safety, or to slash the tires of enemies so that they couldn't escape or give chase. The British Directorate of Military Intelligence Section 9 (MI9), in operation between 1939 and 1945, was known for producing these weapons and distributing them to British agents.

Spy Tools

Espionage gadget development was not restricted to weaponry. Early technologies tended to be large in size. Magnetic tape recorders were new in the 1930s and were bulky objects the size of tables–not easy to transport and certainly not easily hidden. Even decades later, computers were enormous devices that took up entire walls or rooms, not the tiny handheld devices like smartphones that we have now. Yet fancy spy tools abounded during World War II, from cameras small enough to fit in a tobacco pouch to radio receivers

Simple objects such as keys could be used to conceal paper, film, and even weapons and compasses.

small enough to be concealed in a biscuit tin. Ranging from very simple to complex and intricate, these tools helped spies and agents track the movements and plans of the enemy and gain tactical information to tip the balance of power.

Biscuit Tin Radios

Small radio receivers were useful in the camps and at the battlefield so that the military could get news and intercept coded messages. Discretion was key, and soldiers and agents out in the field needed a way to get hold of these devices without anyone knowing. One way was to use a radio made small enough to conceal in a biscuit tin. Biscuits were a common food during the war, so it wasn't unusual for a group to receive tins of biscuits. The radios were small enough to fit in the bottom of the tin, with a little space left at the top for a cardboard covering and some real biscuits put on top to fool anyone who might open the package.

Concealed Communications

For female agents, coded messages could be hidden in something as small as a makeup compact. Code compacts looked just like regular makeup compacts, except the female agent could tip the mirror to a certain angle to be able to reveal a coded message hidden inside. Small objects containing secrets were not just for female spies—men also made use of small spaces, secreting messages and maps away in pipes, shoes, keys, playing cards, chess pieces, gramophone records, and writing utensils. Even fake silver dollars made good hiding places. Such seemingly trivial objects were not readily suspected to contain crucial information.

Compasses were crucial tools for agents, too. If caught and able to escape, a spy needed to be able to quickly determine direction and find the right way to travel. Ordinary citizens didn't wander around carrying compasses, so agents couldn't either. Instead, compasses were hidden in accessories like buttons and brooches. From the outside these objects looked like mere decorations, but the inside contained a life-saving tool.

Hidden Cameras

Practical photography, utilizing glass lenses and film, was still reasonably young in the 1930s, but that didn't stop it from developing as a spy technology. Near the end of the war in 1945, Eastman Kodak developed the Camera-X for the US OSS. Camera-X was small enough to fit in a wooden matchbox, and held enough film to take thirty-four images. Agents could use it fairly easily, but the picture quality wasn't terrific. Still, for an agent needing to snap a couple quick images of documents, it was a useful tool. Typically, the matchbox camera was used by American agents and by members of the resistance in Europe.

The Germans also used a tiny, concealable camera. The model of choice for the Nazis was the Robot Star 50, which came in a few variations. It was small enough to be hidden in a woman's purse.

One of the more creative photography technologies was pigeon photography, which is exactly what it sounds like: photography by pigeons. The birds were outfitted with tiny, lightweight cameras that could take aerial surveillance photos while the birds flew. German apothecary Julius Neubronner came up with the idea in the early 1900s and began developing the technology that would allow the camera to take pictures while the bird flew. Neubronner presented

Surveillance Technology ...but no TVs!

There was a stark difference between the cutting-edge technology used by spies and the military on the battlefield and what was found in common households during World War II. Most people didn't even have a camera. In the modern world video can be streamed twenty-four hours a day, but less than one hundred years ago in 1939, the first commercial black-and-white televisions were demonstrated to the public at the World's Fair in New York. In 1941, there were only ten television stations broadcasting about fifteen hours per week in the United States.

When America entered World War II, commercial production of television sets and radios was banned so that resources could be dedicated to the war effort. At the time, there were only about five thousand televisions in households across the country. For entertainment, most families listened to the radio on average five hours a day.

Full-scale production of televisions commenced in 1947, two years after the end of the war, and Americans were ready to embrace the technology. When the first color programs began to air in 1953, 50 percent of Americans owned a television, amounting to one in each of 25,233,000 homes. Retail sales continued to expand exponentially, and now most Americans find themselves in front of one screen or another at all hours of the day.

his pigeons and the technique to the government during World War I, and the method was used in a couple of battles. However, pigeons weren't widely utilized, despite the fact that test flights showed satisfactory results.

World War II was a different story, though. Carrier pigeons were used extensively. Often the birds were used to carry messages that were placed in a tiny canister strapped to the pigeon. In addition, the Germans worked on training pigeons for aerial photography flights. The Nazi forces also reportedly trained dogs to carry the pigeons in baskets and then release them. It's unknown how many pigeons were ultimately used for aerial photography, but the technology was developed by both the Germans and the French, and multiple armies utilized pigeons to transfer and gather information.

DID YOU KNOW?

Homing pigeons were used to transmit messages and take aerial photographs because they were incredibly reliable at returning to their home location, even over distances of more than a thousand miles.

Cryptography

World War II wasn't just all fun, James Bond–style gadgets for surveillance and protection, though. Cryptography played a huge role, and there were a number of techniques and technologies used to support encrypting and code breaking.

One-Time Pads

One simple yet incredibly effective method of cryptography was the one-time pad (OTP), or single-use encoder pad. The OTP was essentially a technique that could not be cracked, because the codes were generated randomly and only used one time each. The "pad" referred to the early application of the system where a pad was used to write two sheets for each encryption: one for the person encoding the message, and one for the person decoding the message. After the receiver had decoded the message, the sheets would be destroyed and never used again. The next time a coded message needed to be sent, a new code sheet would be used. Leo Marks, the head of the codes office of the British Secret Operations Executive, used this method during the war with overseas operatives and for messages between offices.

Bletchley Park was home to numerous cryptography teams comprised of men and women from a variety of backgrounds.

M-209 Cipher Box

Another practice used for cryptography during World War II was the cipher box. The M-209 cipher box was developed by Swedish inventor Boris Hagelin, embraced by the US Navy, and widely used by the US military. Rotors in the machine would be used to encode and decode communications. The encoder would set the six key wheels on the top of the box to a random sequence of letters, and that would establish the code that would be used for the message. The encoder would have to provide this setting to the decoder for the message to be read, much like the decoder of a message using a single-use encoder pad would need a copy of the pad to decode the message.

However, the M-209 cipher box wasn't flawless. Enemies could sometimes get hold of the initial random sequence of letters, which would allow them to break the code. It is reported that by 1943, Germans were able to read up to 30 percent of the encrypted messages sent by the M-209. Nevertheless, cipher boxes continued to be used. The Germans had their own devices, called the SG-41 and SG-39.

Code Talkers

Just as in World War I, Native Americans were recruited for encryption during World War II. The most famous group from this period are the Navajo, but troops from other tribes were deployed as well, including the Meskwaki, Comanche, and Lakota nations. The code talkers were communications specialists for various branches of the military. Sometimes the soldiers simply translated messages into native dialects, but the languages were also used as the basis for new codes.

The use of Native Americans to encrypt messages was so successful during World War I that Adolf Hitler sent anthropologists to the United States to learn the languages before World War II began, hoping to be able to break future transmissions. As it turned out, there were simply too many languages and dialects for the German anthropologists to learn, and each much too difficult to master in a short period.

Navajo language was particularly well suited for cryptography because it is only spoken, not written—there is no alphabet and there are no symbols. It also has extremely complex syntax and tonal qualities. For non-native speakers of the language, it took a great deal of time and effort just to become partially fluent. When World War II began, it was estimated that fewer than thirty non-Navajos could speak the language.

Amazingly, the Navajo code talkers were faster than the computers of the time, too. In 1942, the military tested Navajo code talkers versus machines and found that the Navajo could encode, transmit,

Members of the Navajo tribe were hugely important to the United States' encoding efforts during World War II.

DID YOU KNOW?

The code developed by the Navajo code talkers was so intricate that even a native Navajo couldn't crack it! A Navajo soldier who was taken prisoner in the Pacific was forced to listen to the code and attempt to break it, but he couldn't do it.

and decode a three-line message in twenty seconds, whereas an encoding device took thirty minutes to do the same thing. After the tests, the Marines began to recruit and train Navajo cryptographers. By the end of the war, approximately 540 Navajo would serve, roughly four hundred of whom worked as code talkers.

Most were sent to the Pacific theater, where tensions were high. The code talkers transmitted information, orders, and other communications and acted as messengers in every battle the US Marines waged in the Pacific theater between 1942 and 1945. They were so effective at their job that Major Howard Connor of the 5th Marine Division stated, "Were it not for the Navajos, the Marines would never have taken Iwo Jima," a major win for the Allies in the Pacific theater. In fact, the six Navajo code talkers working at Iwo Jima transmitted more than eight hundred messages in two days, without a single error!

MAX BLANK
ALFRED E. BROKHOFF
HEINRICH CLAUSING
CONRADINE DOLD
FREDERICK DUQU
HARD EICHENLAUB
HEINRICH CARL EILERS
PAUL FEHSE
EDMUND CARL HEINE
FELIX JAHNKE
OSEF KLEIN
HARTWIG KLEISS
HERMAN LANG
EVELYN CLAYTON LEWIS
RENE EMANUEL MEZ
ERETT ROEDER
PAUL SCHOLZ
GEORGE GOTTLOB SCHUH
ERWIN WILHELM SIEGLER
OSCAR STABLER
ILLY STEIN
FRANZ JOSEPH STIGLER
ERICK STRUNK
LEO WAALEN
ADOLF WALISCHEWS
WHEELER-HILL
BERTRAM W. ZENZINGER
THE
33 CONVICTED MEMBERS
OF THE
DUQUESNE
SPY RING

CHAPTER 3

ACCOMPLISHMENTS IN WORLD WAR II

Leading up to World War II, Japan, Italy, and Germany were involved in various conflicts and had been separately asserting supremacy to expand control over the world; although there were some treaties in place, the situation was precarious. The German invasion of Poland on September 1, 1939, officially marked the start of World War II. Great Britain and France sided with Poland, forming the Allied powers, and thereafter more conflicts and alliances followed. Germany, Japan, and Italy signed the Tripartite Pact in 1940, and were known as the Axis Powers. The British Commonwealth, the Soviet

OPPOSITE:
Thirty-three members of the Duquesne spy ring, led by Frederick Joubert Duquesne, were convicted in 1941 of espionage.

Union, the United States, and China all sided with the Allies.

Nazi Germany had made great technological advancements even before Hitler rose to power in 1933. Under Hitler's rule, antisemitism and the purity of the German race became a focus for a number of German scientists, yet others were developing new military science and techniques. Therefore, the Allies were faced with enormous challenges and had to work smarter, better, and faster to ultimately defeat the Nazis and the Axis countries. That meant spies had to be clever, too, and cryptographers had to develop new, unbreakable codes and code technologies to keep plans secret from the enemy. Both sides raced to outsmart the other and achieve their goal of victory. With major powers vying for control, it's no surprise that espionage, spy technology, and cryptography experienced major improvements during World War II.

Air Reconnaissance

World War II was a turning point for air reconnaissance. As tensions rose before the war, an Australian named Sidney Cotton, working for the British Secret Intelligence Service (MI6), began outfitting planes with hidden cameras so he could shoot aerial photographs discreetly. He created a special camera mount known as the trimetrogon, which allowed pilots to obtain more accurate aerial images of a region. He also pioneered the use of heated cameras for aerial photography, which was an important development because it allowed pilots to shoot pictures from a higher altitude, which had previously been impossible because higher altitudes resulted in the camera lens fogging up.

In the early days of the war, Germany actually had superior optic capabilities to Britain—their camera technology was more advanced. However, Germany did not prioritize aerial reconnaissance nearly as much as the British did, and so the British ultimately overtook them in that area.

Aircraft development was key during World War II, particularly for air combat purposes. For espionage

DID YOU KNOW?

Sidney Cotton was a close friend of British Prime Minister Winston Churchill, a decisive voice in World War II, and Ian Fleming—author of the enormously popular James Bond spy novels!

purposes planes needed to be fast, able to fly high, and capable of covering long distances. Reconnaissance aviators had to fly fast over enemy territory in order to avoid being shot down and also maneuver to capture good pictures. Using new technology, like that developed by Cotton, greatly helped overcome these challenges. The use of infrared film also improved aircraft surveillance. Infrared technology allowed for better camouflage detection by using the nonvisible infrared portion of the light spectrum to take photographs.

American Eyes in the Air

The United States followed Britain's lead on making air reconnaissance a priority, and developed the F-series of

Modern aerial reconnaissance is computerized, but an actual photographer was on board to take images in World War II.

planes for photographic reconnaissance. Not all of the F-series planes were a success in this area, though. The F-4 was somewhat of a failure, and the United States experienced a bit of a setback in aerial reconnaissance before developing the F-5, which proved to be far more reliable and better suited to surveillance than the F-4. They were also keen to use the British de Havilland Mosquito (designated as the F-8 in the American fleet), which was well known as a good reconnaissance aircraft, along with the Spitfire.

Espionage

Spies on the ground continued to uncover and gather secret information, influencing countries' actions in the war. Operations were covert and could involve whole spy rings or individuals. The task was incredibly dangerous; agents could be killed in service or captured, facing imprisonment or even execution.

The Duquesne Ring

One massive spy ring in World War II was known as the Duquesne spy ring. The name came from its leader, Frederick "Fritz" Joubert Duquesne, a United States citizen and Nazi sympathizer. Duquesne was born in South Africa but became a US citizen in 1913. During

World War I, however, he was a spy for Germany, despite being an American citizen. Duquesne was so effective in covering his spy tracks that he was hired as an employee for the US government's Works Progress Administration in 1935.

When World War II broke out, Duquesne established a spy ring to work on behalf of German military intelligence. The spies in the Duquesne ring generally worked in normal jobs that effectively disguised their work as spies. For example, one opened a restaurant and would obtain sensitive information from his customers. Others worked as delivery people, which was the perfect cover for transmitting secret messages. Another worked for an airline and thus had knowledge of which Allied ships were crossing the Atlantic. Still another worked on the docks and thus had similar knowledge of ships leaving for Europe. Many others worked on ships and thus could provide extensive information about shipping, supplies, and naval weaponry to the Germans. An executive in the American automobile industry was recruited as a spy so he could pass secrets about automobiles and aviation to the German military.

All of the members of the spy ring seemed, at first glance, to be average American citizens. All were in position to aid the Germany by providing sensitive information that allowed the Nazis to gain insight into

American strategies and plans. However, the spy ring was brought down by a single recruit, William Sebold.

On a visit to his mother in Germany, Sebold was approached by the Gestapo and infomed that he would provide intelligence to Duquesne upon his return to the United States. Sebold agreed to do so, but when applying for a replacement passport so he could return to the United States (his had been stolen), Sebold confessed to the consulate that he had been recruited as a German spy but that he wished to aid the United States instead. Sebold became a double agent, working for the Federal Bureau of Investigation (FBI). With his help, the FBI was able to capture and sentence thirty-three people involved in the Duquesne spy ring.

Bletchley Park and the Enigma Code

One of the key factors that led the Allies to victory in World War II was the cracking of the Enigma code. Enigma code wasn't just one single code; rather, the term was used to describe a polyalphabetic substitution cipher, where multiple substitution alphabets are used to design a code. That same code wasn't used throughout the war—the cipher could be used over and over to create new substitution codes.

The Enigma Machine

For a code to be truly unbreakable, the key sequences need to be totally random. If humans create a substitution code, there is always some pattern, no matter how hard one tries to keep it random. It's just human nature—our brains think in patterns. That was the beauty of the Enigma code. It was machine-generated, which made each cipher truly random. The electro-mechanical rotor cipher machines were invented by a German engineer, Arthur Scherbius, as World War I ended.

Enigma machines looked like large, boxy typewriters with light-up letters. The cryptographer would start by setting three rotors to predetermined positions. Messages would then be entered by pressing letters on the keyboard, such as A, and one or more of the rotors would rotate. When the rotor would settle into place, it would create a circuit with the other rotors and the fixed electrical wiring in the

Thousands of Enigma machines were used, some like this 1930s model.

DID YOU KNOW?

According to computer expert and Engima historian Ralph Simpson, without the specific rotor settings, it would take 100,000 Enigma operators twice the age of the universe to correctly decipher a message, even if they each worked twenty-four hours a day, testing one setting every second.

device, which would create an electrical pathway to one of the light-up letters, such as X. X would light up on the machine, and thus every time the letter A appeared in the original message, it would appear as an X in the encrypted message. The electrical paths would change each time an encryption was done, which meant the code was truly randomly generated, and thus very hard to crack.

After World War I, German scientists were forbidden to collaborate with scientists from other countries. The German military naturally turned to the Enigma to create coded messages, and started making modifications to the mechanics in order to keep the design unique in the 1920s. Enigma machines were, after all, a German invention. Believing the random nature of Enigma codes to be unbreakable, the Axis powers used the strategy to communicate during World War II, with various versions of the machine in use creating distinct codes amongst the countries and their militaries. However, according to British code breakers working at Bletchley Park, most of the Germans using Enigma did not operate the machine correctly. This vulnerability in the code allowed Allied forces to decrypt and read the intelligence being sent by the Axis powers.

The British Government Code and Cipher School

British, Polish, and French agents worked at Bletchley Park during the war, decrypting Axis code, such as the Engima and Lorenz ciphers. (The Lorenz cipher

Bletchley Park has housed some of the most sophisticated cryptanalysts.

was, like Engima, created by rotor cipher machines that were invented by a German engineer.) Bletchley Park, located north of London, was home to the Government Code and Cipher School (GC&CS) and was the central site for British code breakers during the war. Naturally, the location of Bletchley Park was kept as secret as possible, but it was cleverly located right across from a train station from which trains ran to both Oxford and Cambridge universities—places from where remarkable individuals could be recruited.

The code breakers who worked at Bletchley Park weren't necessarily schooled in cryptography, though. Some were linguists, some were gifted at solving crossword puzzles and anagrams, and others were skilled chess players. People with these backgrounds tended to have the lateral thinking skills that made for good code breakers. Lateral thinkers would be able to approach a seemingly unsolvable problem, like breaking the Enigma, through creative and untraditional methods rather than an obvious logical step-by-step approach.

It wasn't like the GC&CS could just place an ad in the paper looking for potential cryptographers, though. Clever tactics had to be used to find people whose thinking skills would be well suited to the task at hand. For example, the GC&CS once had a local paper feature a cryptic crossword competition. They then obtained the names of people who had done well in the competition and approached them privately to ask if they would be interested in joining the team at Bletchley Park.

One such person was Mavis Batey (nee Lever), a code breaker who helped England win a key 1941 naval victory in the Battle of Cape Matapan by breaking the Italian Engima. Batey was gifted at crosswords and had an innate ability for transposing letters and numbers. She knew instinctively that H was the eighth letter of the alphabet, for example. That ability to transpose automatically made her a prime candidate as a code breaker.

Along with those skilled with letters and words, Commander Alastair Denniston, head of the GC&CS until 1942, recognized that since the Axis were using electromechanical machines, exceptional mathematicians would also be needed. One such individual was Alan Turing, a mathematician thought by many to be the founder of theoretical computer science and artificial intelligence. Turing is credited as helping to break Enigma codes that allowed the Allies to beat the Axis in several critical battles, leading to the eventual defeat of the Axis powers and saving an estimated fourteen million lives.

breaker who worked at Bletchley Park during World War II until his death in 1943.

Some of the women (known as Dilly's girls), like Mavis Batey, were chosen for their logical mind and potential as code breakers. Others, like Margaret Rock, were mathematicians. Normally, women in that era rarely got the opportunity to pursue degrees in STEM fields (science, technology, engineering, and mathematics), but with many men fighting in the war, women had more opportunity to enter universities and pursue higher education. Like Batey, Rock was part of Dilly Knox's team, and she and Batey ultimately broke the Abwehr Enigma machine (a German Enigma machine).

Many of the female code breakers at Bletchley Park worked in Hut 6.

American Code Breakers

While cracking Enigma and Lorenz codes was crucial to the success of the Allies in World War II, these were not the only ciphers that code breakers were working on. The United States had multiple agencies working intelligence. The US Army's Signal Intelligence Service (SIS) and the US Office of Chief of Naval Operations, 20th Division of the Office of Naval Communications, G Section / Communications Security (OP-20-G) had been deciphering coded messages since before the war. Once Japan bombed Pearl Harbor, the United States military focused even more resources towards breaking codes.

Thanks to the efforts of cryptanalysts, the Battle of Midway was ultimately a huge victory for the Allies.

While the Germans used mechanical ciphers like the Enigma and Lorenz machines, the Japanese used book ciphers. These are exactly what they sound like: Encryption is done by looking up codes in a book, and deciphering by the recipient is done in the same way—by cross-referencing a code book. In a way it's a simpler cipher technique than the Enigma, but it was also relatively difficult to break. They used both random numbers and characters from the Japanese writing system. They also used a technique called superencipherment, where the code groups themselves are also enciphered—a code within a code.

Station HYPO and the Battle of Midway

OP-20-G code breakers at Station HYPO, the decryption center at Pearl Harbor, Hawaii, headed by Captain Joseph Rochefort, had to strip out the superencipherment and then break down the code groups. They did so by cross-referencing code usage in other messages, as well as using punch-card sorting machines created by IBM to find messages in the specific code groups. The punch-card data was stored in a massive card catalog of deductions about JN-25 code groups (the name the United States had given to Japanese naval codes).

Months after the Japanese bombed Pearl Harbor, HYPO code breakers were able to decipher radio messages indicating that the Japanese were planning another attack in the Central Pacific, but they were unsure where. OP-20-G had multiple stations working on encrypted messages; some cryptanalysts thought it might be another attack on Hawaii, while others felt it would be at Midway Island. The Japanese were simply referring to their target as AF. Code breakers were also unsure of the date, though they deduced from coded messages that it would be sometime in May or June of 1942.

Jasper Homes at HYPO is credited with the deceptively simply plan to determine where the attack would take place. The station secretly communicated to Midway (via an underwater communications cable that the Japanese could not break) to broadcast via radio a message that Midway's desalinization plant had failed. They instructed Midway to broadcast the message with no encryption, so that the Japanese would be sure to understand it. As expected, the Japanese listened to the radio message and then sent an encoded message that AF's desalinization plant had failed. When Station HYPO code breakers intercepted the Japanese message and decoded it, they finally had confirmation that AF was indeed Midway Island.

Cryptanalysts at HYPO also broke the date encryption on Japanese messages, and were able to narrow down the time and enable US forces to be better prepared for the attack. In the end, the Battle of Midway was a decisive victory for the Allies, who were able to destroy much of the Japanese fleet. In fact, although the war continued after the Battle of Midway, Midway is considered to be one of the most stunning defeats in naval warfare history and a turning point in the war.

The Invasion of Normandy

The largest amphibious military operation in history, and a deciding battle in World War II, is widely recognized as the invasion of Normandy on June 6, 1944. Code named D-Day, this Allied victory was achieved through large-scale intelligence planning and the success of a deception strategy called Operation Bodyguard.

The principal aim of Bodyguard was to misdirect the Axis forces and ensure Germany would not increase military strength in the area by giving false signals that the Allies were attacking other locations. The plan was immense and involved multiple operations, each with its own code name, and numerous spies, double agents, and cryptographers contributing an enormous amount of work. False radio transmissions were made, and in some cases, mock military equipment, like tanks and landing craft, were also fabricated for visual deception.

Ultimately the Allies prevailed over Germany, and though a few battles followed D-Day, on May 7, 1945, Germany surrendered, ending World War II in Europe. In August the United States escalated attacks on Japan, dropping atomic bombs on the cities of Hiroshima and Nagasaki. By September the largest world war to date came to an end.

Formalized American Intelligence

Prior to World War II, intelligence operations in the United States had been conducted as needed by various departments, like the State and Treasury. Both the Army and Navy also had cryptography units. The activities carried out by these independent agencies were not necessarily coordinated. This would change after June 14, 1942, when under order of President Franklin D. Roosevelt, a new agency was formed.

The Office of Strategic Services (OSS) was established to coordinate intelligence and espionage efforts for the US Armed Forces, and was inspired by the coordinated British agencies Secret Intelligence Service (MI6) and Special Operations Executive (SOE). In fact, it was the suggestion of William Stephenson, a senior British intelligence officer, that motivated Roosevelt to request a plan for a new organization.

Britain's MI6 was established in 1909 and is a British national security agency that still exists. The SOE, on the other hand, existed only from 1940 to 1946. It was put in place to conduct espionage in occupied Europe during World War II and to help resistance movements against the Axis powers. Several months after the war was over, the agency was dissolved. The OSS was dissolved at the end of the war but eventually became what is now known as the Central Intelligence Agency, or CIA.

New York World-Telegram
NIGHT
NAZIS GIVE UP
SURRENDER TO ALLIES
AND RUSSIA ANNOUNCED
SURRENDER TO ALLIES
AND RUSSIA ANNOUNCED

CHAPTER 4

THE IMPACT OF INTELLIGENCE

World War II got more public attention and media coverage than earlier wars. Certainly the conflict involved all of the world's powerful countries, but a large reason for the increase in reporting was because technology had improved greatly in the twentieth century. Television still wasn't an everyday household appliance, but radio was a prominent form of communication, and people were also able to read about the war in newspapers and periodicals. Information traveled much faster and reached a wider audience than it could during World War I. Civilians around the world were aware

OPPOSITE:
The growing news media made the actions of code breakers and spies accessible to the public.

of the major events and issues of the war, including the espionage and cryptography advancements that had been made.

Espionage and cryptography operations, by their very nature, were kept largely under wraps, but pieces of information were shared, and the public knew that these things existed. Civilians might not know the specifics of how spies obtained and transmitted information, or the methods code breakers used to decrypt messages, but the public knew numerous covert efforts were impacting the war. Some innovations and operations have been touched on here, but even today more information is revealed about intelligence undertakings during World War II. These efforts had a lasting impact on culture and shaped future developments both in those areas and for civilian life as well.

Spies in Popular Culture

Espionage has long been fascinating to the public. In fact, the first American spy novel is thought to have been *The Spy,* by James Fenimore Cooper, published in 1821. However, many other espionage-related books, movies, and television shows have followed. On the surface, being a spy seems like an exciting departure from the everyday lives of most people—going behind enemy lines, donning a disguise, and transmitting secret messages that can change the outcome of conflicts. That sort of life makes for interesting stories in movies, literature, and television.

Bond, James Bond

One of the most famous spies in literature and movies is undoubtedly James Bond. The fictional character was created by novelist Ian Fleming. Fleming wrote twelve books and two short-story collections featuring Bond, published between 1953 and his death in 1964. Several other authors have since picked up the torch and written novels featuring Bond, and the character has been portrayed in numerous movies, television shows, radio shows, comic strips, and video games.

Madame Tussaud's wax gallery has immortalized in wax the actors who have played James Bond on film.

It is safe to say it is James Bond that comes to mind when most people envision a spy.

The fictitious James Bond is an agent for the British MI6 intelligence agency. Fleming stated that he created the character based on a number of agents he worked with while he was in the Naval Intelligence Division during World War II, one of whom was his own brother. He also drew upon his own personality traits and his experiences in intelligence.

Particularly in the films, Bond used spy technology and gadgets, though generally his success is due to Bond's own abilities as a spy. Still, given that spy technologies such as hidden cameras, secret microphones, and increasingly sophisticated surveillance technology were developed during World War II, it seems appropriate that Bond and his adversaries would be outfitted with some sort of gadgetry—even if it was perhaps a bit embellished to appeal to movie audiences!

DID YOU KNOW?

James Bond has been portrayed in movies by seven actors so far. The first was Sean Connery, in six films. The actor to play Bond in the most films as of 2017 is Roger Moore, whose seven films were released in the 1970s and 1980s.

The Cold War began roughly a decade after World War II ended, and so many plotlines in books, movies, and television moved toward Cold War espionage. Although James Bond was born from World War II, the novels were set in the contemporary period of the 1950s and 1960s. The films overtly used the Cold War era as the setting, starting right from the release of the first film, *Dr. No*, in 1962.

The Cold War, Espionage, and Everyday Life

Part of the legacy of World War II was the Cold War, although it wasn't an outright physical war like previous conflicts. Instead, it was a state of geographical tension, involving espionage, psychological warfare, propaganda, and proxy wars spanning more than four decades.

After World War II, the world was left with two superpowers: the United States and the Soviet Union. The two forces had been united in their fight against Nazi Germany and Hitler's takeover, but when the war ended and Hitler was defeated, the nations found themselves at odds. The United States was a society of capitalism and democracy, whereas the Soviet Union was a communist power. The Cold War centered on

The USSR made public displays of military strength including ballistic missiles.

the political and economic differences between the two nations, with other countries falling on one side or the other.

Along with the United States were the countries allied under the North Atlantic Treaty Organization (NATO) in 1949, referred to as the Western Bloc. The Soviet Union and other nations in Eastern and Central Europe formally announced their alliance with the Warsaw Pact in 1955. Both wanted to see their respective views about society spread, and prevent the spread of the other philosophy.

Perhaps what truly motivated the Cold War was the fear of nuclear warfare. Both superpowers continued to further develop their nuclear technology, operating under the belief that as long as each had equal capabilities neither would risk the devastation sure to follow if the weapons were launched. The espionage and cryptology methods and technologies that evolved in the first part of the twentieth century became the principal defenses and weapons of the Cold War.

Atomic Spies

Joseph Stalin was in power in the Soviet Union from 1922 until 1952; when World War II ended he was determined to keep pace with the United States where nuclear weapons were concerned, and he expanded the Soviet spy network to gather intelligence. Although not formerly an organized spy ring, these agents are often referred to as atomic spies, and one of their major targets was the Manhattan Project.

The United States' top secret project to develop nuclear weapons, done in conjunction with the United Kingdom and Canada, took place at numerous facilities. The facility at Los Alamos, New Mexico, was reportedly full of Soviet spies, and many secrets were stolen. One female agent actually smuggled out plans for the atomic bomb in an unremarkable tissue box! It's thought that the leaks of confidential information about nuclear weapons smuggled to the Soviet Union were significant and ultimately saved the Soviet atomic team years in development time.

Red Scare

Numerous suspected Soviet spies were tried and convicted during the Cold War era. For example, Julius and Ethel Rosenberg were a married couple thought to have smuggled sensitive information about nuclear development to the KGB, the Soviet Union's intelligence agency during the Cold War. The arrest of the Rosenbergs was covered in the media and they were certainly not alone: many other co-conspirators and spies were arrested and tried as well, leading governments and civilians alike to wonder how many more agents remained in secret. This fear rose to a red scare.

The Rosenbergs were executed in 1953 for committing espionage.

A red scare is any widespread paranoia of the spread of communism; one occurred during World War I, but in the decade following World War II there was a pronounced red scare in the United States, thanks to Senator Joseph McCarthy and the House Un-American Activities Committee (HUAC). Senator McCarthy launched a campaign spreading fear among the American public and accused many of espionage and treason, often without any evidence. His crusade is commonly referred to as McCarthyism.

During the McCarthy era Americans were subjected to constant messages portraying the image that not only was the country under threat of nuclear war from across the sea, but that Red agents were everywhere. HUAC was formed to hold hearings regarding espionage activities, and when members of the Communist Party of the United States of America (CPUSA) and other spies testified in front of the HUAC that spies had infiltrated the US government, it further stoked the panic.

Before long, anyone who Senator McCarthy or HUAC thought might have connections to communism became suspect, and many were called to testify in front of HUAC. Famously, a number of celebrities in Hollywood were called in front of the committee, including screenwriters, authors, actors, singers, and musicians. Perhaps the most famous name of the Hollywood accused was the much-loved Lucille Ball. Ball had registered to vote as a member of the Communist Party in the 1930s, at her grandfather's request. However, when called before HUAC, she affirmed that she had never actually voted communist and that she had never had any intention of doing

Numerous Hollywood writers and producers were called in front of the HUAC as part of the Red Scare.

so. Thus, Ball avoided being blacklisted like some of her Hollywood colleagues were.

As unbelievable as the unfounded accusations and acts motivated by fear may sound now, McCarthyism and the Red Scare were big problems in the post–World War II United States. Americans were still reeling from World War II and living in fear of another world war—this time with the Soviet Union. When someone pointed fingers at people as being Red or affiliated with communism in any way, it created distrust and division in American society.

Espionage and Surveillance of Citizens

The rise of espionage in World War II made one thing very clear: anyone could be a spy. Your next-door neighbor or an unassuming bakery owner might be secretly transmitting sensitive information to the enemy. Spies weren't just high-level government employees or trained operatives; a spy could be anyone. For this reason, many countries began to keep track of the activities of their citizens.

This was not necessarily a new practice for governments. Hitler did the same thing when he forced Jews to wear gold stars on their clothes—it was a way of keeping tabs on the people he thought needed to be watched. Hitler also controlled the media in Germany so that citizens received only the news and information that he wanted them to receive. This was another way of controlling citizens and keeping an eye on what they knew. Stalin used some similar tactics for controlling Soviet citizens in the post–World War II era.

Certainly, not all countries went as far as Hitler. Watching and then targeting a particular ethnic or religious group for destruction is genocide, and while Hitler's Germany is not the only country in history to have done this, it's not a common or accepted practice. Yet keeping an eye on citizens of concern is—it was done before World War II, during World War II, and it continues to be done to this day.

Surveillance Technology

Surveillance today has become much more high-tech than it was in World War II, though. In the war era, people were physically followed by agents, and perhaps their homes or workplaces were bugged with listening devices. Nowadays, though, such techniques seem simplistic—technology has moved far beyond that.

Law enforcement agencies install security cameras to monitor traffic or watch for potential crimes.

Data and electronic surveillance is far more common now. In a digital era, just about every piece of data about a person is accessible. The United States government, for example, keeps tabs on citizens through the National Security Agency (NSA), which performs electronic surveillance on citizens by tracking internet communications, among other tactics. The NSA's goal is to track potential terrorists—those inside the United States who may be communicating with terrorist cells outside the United States.

Eyes Everywhere

During World War II, the Office of Censorship was created to monitor mail communication, particularly among the sixteen thousand people on the US Censorship Watchlist. It was a big job, and at its peak fifteen thousand people worked to review mail communications. The Office of Censorship was disbanded after the war, but the NSA is

Cryptography in the Digital Era

The rise in surveillance and advancements in digital technology have actually made code breaking and cryptography a big part of modern life. Agencies and businesses encrypt sensitive data to protect it, such as banks encrypting citizens' financial and personal information to prevent fraud and identity theft. Government agencies encrypt sensitive data as well—for obvious reasons. Yet hackers are very skilled at breaking encryption and gaining access to sensitive information and data. Banks and stores frequently experience data breaches, and government agencies are far from immune. Sometimes, the government steps in and insists that companies break encryption and share private information, such as when the FBI ordered Apple Computer to release data from the iPhone used by a terrorist who carried out an attack in San Bernardino, California.

essentially performing the same function—just with electronic communications.

Further, some countries establish watchlists of potential threats to national security—including the United States. In the post–World War II years, Project Shamrock and Project Minaret, both created by the government, monitored communications of American citizens and created watchlists of potential threats. Both programs were shut down in the 1970s, but similar surveillance persists today. For example, the Transportation Security Administration (TSA) has watchlists of potential terrorists, and the people on those watchlists are screened with extra care every time they enter or exit the country.

This surveillance has a goal of national security, as governments claim the actions are done to protect citizens by keeping tabs on potential threats. Indeed, many would agree that this is a valid concern. However, civilian surveillance has had a lasting impact on society and culture as well. Innocent citizens have found themselves caught in the crosshairs of surveillance and labeled as threats when they weren't. Martin Luther King, Jr., for example, was on the national security watchlist. So were actress Jane Fonda and boxer Muhammad Ali.

To try to prevent the NSA from overstepping its boundaries with regard to surveillance of private citizens, the Senate created the Foreign Intelligence Surveillance Act (FISA) in 1978, which enforces stricter regulations for NSA surveillance. FISA has been amended several times since the 1970s, but it still exists as a protection on citizens' right to privacy from NSA surveillance.

The Age of WikiLeaks

In the modern day, technology has allowed espionage to become very public. In the past, a communication might be infiltrated and shared, but it was not to the mass public at large. Now, with the internet present nearly everywhere, sensitive information can be shared with just a few keystrokes.

WikiLeaks is probably the best-known site for the sharing of sensitive information. It was founded by Julian Assange in 2006, and since then has posted millions of classified, sensitive, and secret documents and information provided by anonymous sources. The site has published confidential documents regarding military activities in the Middle East, classified documents from the US State Department, and secret files about prisoners being held at a federal detention center.

In 2016, WikiLeaks was heavily in the news when it published emails and other documents that were damaging to the reputation of presidential candidate Hillary Clinton. It is thought that the site obtained these emails and documentation from Russian hackers (some speculate in collusion with President Trump's campaign team, in an attempt to derail Clinton's campaign), but the truth on that may never be known, since WikiLeaks documents are often obtained from anonymous sources.

WikiLeaks and similar sites have taken espionage into the public domain in a way it never was in World War II.

Chronology

1926 German navy adopts the Enigma cipher machine.

1938 England's Bletchley Park is established as a center for intelligence and cryptography as tensions mount in Europe.

1939 World War II begins when Germany invades Poland. Bletchley Park's Alan Turing cracks the German Enigma code for naval indicator systems.

1940 Britain's Prime Minister Winston Churchill sets up the Special Operations Executive (SOE). Mavis Batey is recruited to work at Bletchley Park, as one of "Dilly's girls."

1941 President Franklin D. Roosevelt creates the Office of the Coordinator of Information: the first peacetime, civilian intelligence agency. Bletchley Park's Mavis Batey helps break the Abwehr Enigma, leading to an important victory for the Allies.

Dec. 1941 The Japanese bomb Pearl Harbor, in the United States' most costly intelligence disaster.

1942 President Roosevelt splits the Office of the Coordinator of Information into two branches and establishes the Office of Strategic Services (OSS), which later becomes today's Central Intelligence Agency (CIA), and the Office of War

Information (OWI). US military recruits Navajo code talkers, after learning that they are faster cryptographers than even computers. The SOE begins recruiting women.

June 1942 The Battle of Midway takes place—a victory for the United States thanks to US Navy code breakers.

1943 Italy surrenders to the Allies—the first of the Axis Powers to do so.

June 1944 Allied troops successfully invade Normandy, France, thanks to the effective strategy of Operation Bodyguard.

May 1945 Germany surrenders to the Allies.

Aug. 1945 The United States drops atomic bombs on the Japanese cities of Hiroshima and Nagasaki.

Sept. 1945 Japan surrenders to the Allies.

Glossary

anagram Word or phrase formed by rearranging the letters of another word or phrase.

apothecary An old name for a person who prepared and sold medications.

artificial intelligence The use of computers to perform tasks that normally require human intelligence.

capitalism An economic and political system where trade is controlled by private owners for profit.

cipher A code or a way of writing code.

communism A political system in which all property is publicly owned and people are paid according to their abilities and needs.

cryptography The art of writing and solving codes. Cryptographers write codes, cryptanalysts study and break them.

democracy A system of government in which all citizens have a voice, usually through elected representatives.

dirigible An airship, usually with a rigid structure, that can be steered. A zeppelin is also a rigid airship.

double agent A person who pretends to be a spy for one country but who is really a spy for that country's enemy.

fixed-wing aircraft Aircraft, such as planes, that have fixed wings, as opposed to spinning rotors found on helicopters.

genocide Deliberate killing of a specific group of people, usually of a particular race or ethnic group.

Gestapo German secret police in Nazi Germany.

linguist A person who studies language.

Pacific theater A key area during World War II where many military events occurred. The region included most of the Pacific Ocean and its islands. The attacks on Pearl Harbor and Hiroshima were both in the Pacific theater.

propaganda The publication or distribution of information that is biased or misleading.

reconnaissance Military observation of an area to gain strategic information.

surveillance Close observation.

Further Information

Books

Dignman, Roger. *Deciphering the Rising Sun: Navy and Marine Corps Codebreakers, Translators and Interpreters in the Pacific War.* Annapolis, MD: Naval Institute Press, 2009.

Dunlop, Tessa. *The Bletchley Girls.* London: Hodder & Stoughton, 2015.

Goodman, Michael E. *World War II Spies.* Mankato, MN: Creative Paperbacks, 2016.

Kagan, Neil, and Stephen G. Hyslop. *The Secret History of World War II: Spies, Code Breakers, and Covert Operations.* Des Moines, IA: National Geographic, 2016.

McKay, Sinclair. *The Secret Lives of Codebreakers: The Men and Women Who Cracked the Enigma Code at Bletchley Park.* New York: Plume, 2012.

Websites

BBC: World War II

http://www.bbc.co.uk/history/worldwars/wwtwo/

BBC has an robust page on World War II history that contains links to a great deal of information about the people and events of the war.

History of American Intelligence

https://www.cia.gov/kids-page/6-12th-grade/operation-history/history-of-american-intelligence.html

The CIA hosts a webpage with the history of American intelligence up through World War II.

History of the CIA

https://www.cia.gov/kids-page/6-12th-grade/operation-history/history-of-the-cia.html

The CIA also hosts a page dedicated to the history of the United States' top intelligence agency.

MI5 Security Service: World War II

https://www.mi5.gov.uk/world-war-ii

The UK's MI5 Security Service maintains a World War II espionage page that contains useful information and links to further information on specific events and key people in the war.

Selected Bibliography

Egan, Siobhan. "Civil War Spy Tools." People of Our Everyday Life. http://peopleof.oureverydaylife.com/civil-war-spy-tools-10971.html.

"Espionage Timelines." Timelines. http://timelinesdb.com/listevents.php?subjid=749&title=Espionage.

Hautala, Laura. "Enigma: Why the Fight to Break Nazi Encryption Still Matters." CNet. Jun 6, 2017. https://www.cnet.com/news/enigma-why-the-fight-to-break-nazi-encryption-still-matters/.

Hertling, Mark. "Why the Military Uses 'Blimps.'" CNN. Oct 30, 2015. http://www.cnn.com/2015/10/30/opinions/hertling-why-military-uses-blimps/index.html.

"Infrared Aerial Photography." Aerial Archives. http://www.aerialarchives.com/Infrared-Aerial-Photography.htm.

"Interpreting the Meaning of Infrared Colors." Aerial Archives. http://www.aerialarchives.com/infraredcolors.htm.

Keegan, John. *The Second World War.* New York: Penguin, 2005.

King, Melanie. "Thanks for the Spycraft, World War I." Boston Globe. Aug 3, 2014. https://www.bostonglobe.com/ideas/2014/08/02/thanks-for-spycraft-world-war/lrjmteHDfRevXdP9qGACHN/story.html.

Macintyre, Ben. "Bond—the Real Bond." *The Times.* Apr 5, 2008.

McKay, Sinclair. "Telegraph Crossword: Cracking Hobby Won the Day." The Telegraph. Aug 26, 2010. http://www.telegraph.co.uk/lifestyle/wellbeing/7966268/Telegraph-crossword-Cracking-hobby-won-the-day.html.

"MCR-1." Crypto Museum. http://www.cryptomuseum.com/spy/mcr1/.

"Morse Code and the Telegraph." History.com. http://www.history.com/topics/inventions/telegraph.

"Native Words, Native Warriors." National Museum of the American Indian. http://www.nmai.si.edu/education/codetalkers/html/.

"Navajo Code Talkers: World War II Fact Sheet." Naval History and Heritage Command. https://www.history.navy.mil/research/library/online-reading-room/title-list-alphabetically/n/code-talkers.html.

"Overview of Civil War Codes and Ciphers." Cryptiana. http://cryptiana.web.fc2.com/code/civilwar0.htm.

Watkins, Thayer. "Code Breaking and the Battle of Midway Island." http://www.sjsu.edu/faculty/watkins/midwaybattle.htm.

"Women Codebreakers." Bletchley Park Research. http://www.bletchleyparkresearch.co.uk/research-notes/women-codebreakers/.

Zetter, Kim. "Tools of the Tradecraft: The CIA's Historic Spy Kit." Wired. Feb 24, 2011. https://www.wired.com/2011/02/cia-tools-of-tradecraft/.

Index

About the Author

Cathleen Small is a writer and editor based in the San Francisco Bay Area. Small has written dozens of books for students in grades three through twelve, including biographies of noteworthy women in history and numerous books on wartime technology. When she's not writing or editing, Small enjoys traveling to historical sites and National Parks with her husband and two young sons.